CW00894311

A STORY OF LEAGUE-TOPPING FOOTBALL ANTICS

RAVE BOOKS

Score-Dom loved football.

But none of his friends did.

So he played with himself.

In the street, of all places.

Just dribbling.

That's just what he was doing one Thursday, when he was spotted by a Talent Scout.

"Would you like to play for me?" asked the Talent Scout.

"Wot?" said Score-Dom.

"There's an opening at Arsenil," said the Talent Scout. "Training starts Monday."

On Monday Score-Dom met Rick Rubbins,
the Arsenil Manager.

"I make the lads 'ere 'ard," said Rubbins.

"WOT!" exclaimed Score-Dom.

"I'll make you 'ard too," said Rubbins.
"So you'll get used to rough play."

"Cor," said Score-Dom.

"Well," thought Score-Dom, contentedly,

"I'll never have to play with myself again."

Rick Rubbins thought it was great.

And let Score-Dom hold his trophy.

And guess what?

Arsenil won!

Two – Nil.

Thanks to Score-Dom.

Within minutes he was at it again…

Superb build up. Hard tackle. Thrusting himself
forward he split the Raver's defence wide open.

His muscles hardened with the effort.
And then, with the whole weight of his body,
he shot powerfully.

The ball slammed into the goal mouth.

Score-Dom's head dropped.
He'd scored! Again! Twice in one day!

What a feeling!

Score-Dom was absolutely magnificent.

All his team mates jumped him,
kissing him passionately.

Score-Dom had scored!

Suddenly Arsenil took control.

Score-Dom spotted an opening.
He pressed forward, dribbling like mad.

Legs pumping furiously, he pushed up into
the Bristol area, trying hard not to lose control.

His groin was straining with the effort.

He twitched left. Then right.
A quick flick... and it was there!

GOAL!!!

Bristol Ravers won the toss and kicked off.

The first few minutes were unbelievable.

The Ravers were all over them, probing deep into Arsenil's box.

But Arsenil defended.

And stopped them from shooting.

Two weeks later, it was FA Cup Final day.
Arsenil were playing Bristol Ravers.

"Remember lads this is the FA Cup,"
said Rick Rubbins.

"What's the FA Cup, boss?" asked Score-Dom.

"It's... errr. Two big words. Don't worry about it.
Just remember, the team with the most goals
wins," Rubbins replied.

So, Score-Dom was now a professional footballer.
He had lots of money too.

He got some designer suits (by Armani).

A very fast sports car (by Ferrari).

And a blonde girlfriend (called Mandi).

"After me," said Rubbins. And he burst into song.

"HERE...WE...GO.., HERE...WE...GO..,
HERE WE GO.., HERE WE..."

The lads joined in... "HERE...WE...GO...
HERE..WE..GO.. HERE WE GO – OHH!"

Soon they all had the hang of it.

Soon it was bath time.

Score-Dom jumped in the tub with the rest
of the team.

"RIGHT LADS," said Rick Rubbins forcefully.
"It's the Cup Final in two weeks, and you need
to get one thing right on the day."

So Score-Dom got stuck in.

Throbby Ballton saw him coming.

But he still went down on Score-Dom's tackle.

"GREAT STUFF," shouted Rubbins,
as he cheered them both on.

What fun!

And Score-Dom's ball control was great.

"What's your tackle like lad?" Rubbins continued.
"I like lads with 'ard tackle."

"I'm workin' on it," said Score-Dom.

"Show me what you've got then lad,"
said Rubbins, eagerly.

"Wot now?" asked Score-Dom nervously.

"Aye lad," said Rubbins. "Throbby Ballton's over
there. See if you can get your tackle in on 'im."